Kenneth's 12 Words with 26 Phonics

Written by Elaine Chaffer
Illustrated by Kenneth Chaffer

Kenneth's 12 Words with 26 Phonics

©2025 Elaine Chaffer

No part of this book may be reproduced, stored in a retrieval system, or transmitted in any form or by any means- electronic, mechanical, photocopying, recording, or otherwise- without prior written permission from the publisher, except for brief quotations in reviews or articles.

Published by first26sounds

First published March 2025

ISBN: 9781763615502

Cover design by Kenneth Chaffer

There are 26 letters in the English Alphabet

5 vowels + 21 consonants

In the story of "Kenneth's Cricket Rap"

vowels are coloured green
consonants black
consonant digraphs magenta
(with 1 exception qu)

Kenneth's 12 words contain 26 phonics

Start decoding words by sounding vowels first
consonants next and then the consonant digraphs

Reading is like putting the pieces of a jigsaw together.

Have fun with Kenneth's words!

Visit our website:
www.kennethsrap.com

hand

leg

fox

fox

velvet

buttons

jacket

squid

This is Kenneth

and
this is
his
cricket
rap.

Kenneth is at the test match munching on his chips,

sitting with him is Min checking on the statistics.

Pat is the batsman with his test cap on,

his sixth hit is big and it adds six runs.

The next batsman with the yips has his knickers in knots,

until his quick shot is smashed and his grin expands.

When Josh hits the stumps with his leg spin at the jack,

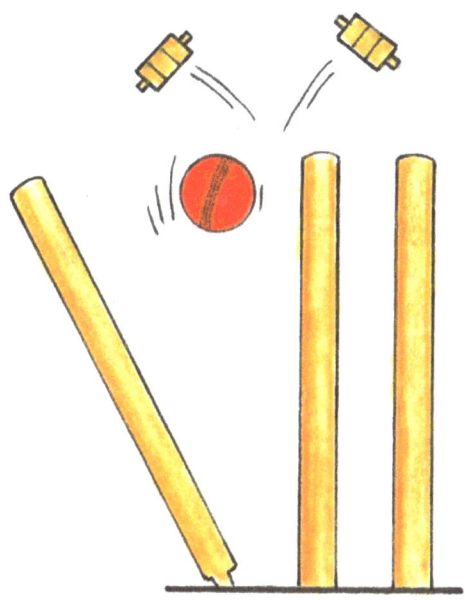

the tenth wicket drops and the test match ends.

Kenneth often visits the M.C.G. and "drinks in" the buzz of the cricket community.

M.C.G. Melbourne Cricket Ground – Sports Stadium in Melbourne, Victoria, Australia

Congratulations on reading:

5 vowels

21 consonants

+ consonant digraphs

Pat on the back!

a	e	i
st**a**nd	n**e**ck	f**i**st

o	u	consonant digraph
pocket	thumb	phonic

www.ingramcontent.com/pod-product-compliance
Lightning Source LLC
Chambersburg PA
CBHW041527070526
44585CB00003B/111